FLY BOY

NAVY WINGS and WILLING WOMEN -WWII

GEORGE A. EDDY, Lt. USNR (fmr)

Outskirts Press, Inc.
Denver, Colorado

Fly Boy
Navy Wings and Willing Women - WWII
All Rights Reserved
Copyright © 2007 George A. Eddy

Outskirts Press
http://www.outskirtspress.com

ISBN-10: 1-59800-734-3
ISBN-13: 978-1-59800-734-3

Outskirts Press and the "OP" logo are trademarks belonging to
Outskirts Press, Inc.
Printed in the United States of America

INTRODUCTION

Every time I watch a rerun of "Victory at Sea" or "The Battle for Midway" on television, I think of World War II and quietly honor the Navy and the pilots involved. I especially relive the TV history of the aircraft carrier INTREPID, called "the finest ship in the Navy". Senator John McCain was stationed on this ship when it was deployed off Viet Nam.

I flew an F4U fighter off the INTREPID near the end of the war in 1945, after it had been hard hit by the enemy and restored to service - twice!

Although there was no combat for my squadron, I spent nearly four years as a Naval Aviator. I was lucky. God was my co-pilot then, in some dicey situations, and still is.

But what I am going to focus on is the lighter side of wartime life, the complex experience of learning to fly a variety of training and operational planes, plus some unusual adventures on land, including memorable romances and finally my rather difficult and creative courtship of a beautiful young woman – one who has stayed with me ever since.

Remember... this was over 60 years ago, in between "Hell's Angels" and "Top Gun". Many of our generation have made their last landing, but these stories may have a continuing life of their own.

I hope you enjoy the journey.

* * * * *

On Sunday December 7th, 1941 I was enjoying a brunch on the Near North side of Chicago. My date was Jackie, a gorgeous blond with a sexy smile and long legs. The night before, she snuggled and squeezed and said, "We are so good together, I think we should have an affair". At age 21, in those olden days, I wasn't sure just what an affair might involve, but any arrangement with her would be fabulous. The party of a half-dozen couples was really festive with Bloody Marys and big band tunes on the Victrola - until a neighbor burst in and said, " Turn on the radio. The Japs just bombed Pearl Harbor! "

The next day I went to the Navy Recruiting Office in Evanston and volunteered to become a pilot. Sadly, I flunked the basic eye test. Like millions of others, I desperately wanted to fly. Pilots commanded respect and romance. So, it was down the hall to the Army Air Corps. Strangely, I passed their more rigorous eye exam, saying I would return for the full physical the next day, Then I marched back to the Navy, which was really my objective. I fancied the sea as exciting and the dark blue uniforms were stylish.

I told the doctor I had just passed the Army eye test and watched as his competitive spirit kicked in. He said maybe he could arrange more light and give me another chance. He twisted a desk lamp so it shone on the chart...and I passed! The full physical was a snap.

The Department of the Navy promptly told me to "stand by" for orders to active duty.

I thought it would be a matter of days. After all, we were suddenly in a full-scale war and the country was certainly not fully prepared. Jackie and I each had studio apartments in the same building, and with my probable short stint as a civilian, we felt one was enough. We saved some money, and the romance was beautiful for young twenty year olds

In the months before the devastating and unexpected attack on Pearl, there were many significant "dots", and like our 9/11disaster in 2001, they weren't connected.

Japan was running out of room and wanted to expand their territory. They invaded Manchuria. In passing, they sunk the US gunship Panay on the Yangtze River in December 1937 ('by mistake" they said - with later apology), and planned to make the Pacific a Japanese Sea.

President Roosevelt cut their import of American oil to 20% of normal, then to zero. We had ample oil in those days! He sent the US Fleet from California to Hawaii. Many historians felt he was enticing action from the Japs - in order to build popular support at home for the war in Europe.

He sent a last minute negotiating letter to Emperor Hirohito, but it may not have been delivered as Admiral Tojo was in total command and already on his way to strike.

We broke the latest Jap code just days before the attack. Whether both Admiral Kimmel and General Short in Honolulu got the word is not known. The word was that the major Jap Fleet was already just days from Hawaii!

This is hindsight of course. All I knew was that our country had been blind-sided and I wanted to fight back. Finally, after six months of restless civilian work, the call came. They needed me! Report to the Naval Air Station, Glenview IL, just outside Chicago.

*   *   *   *   *

Our class of forty was mostly from Northwestern University and was appropriately called the "Flying Wildcats". We each started as lowly Seaman 2nd Class at $21/ month. After 30 days we became, with some pride, Aviation Cadets at $75/ month!

The "Flying Wildcats" were the first class to complete the full primary training syllabus - approximately 100 flying hours - at Glenview. And we were the last to skip "pre-flight" training, three months of intense physical conditioning at a college base. For our group, getting into first class shape involved a little touch football, some ju-jitsu where we learned how to punch our knuckles into the bottom of the adversary's nose, step on his toes, and kick him in the balls...and frequent strenuous liberties, some overnight. Glenview was like a college campus, very laid back. The transition from civilian to military life was slow and easy. Our program took 3 months and led to some very amusing experiences in Chicago\

Our summer dress uniform was like the officers whites, with the choke collar, buttons down the front, and shoulder boards. The insignia for an Aviation Cadet was - one gold star on the traditional black shoulder board. On liberty in the city where the Navy had not been seen a great deal, we were saluted by almost everyone in uniform, often by Army Sergeants with hash marks showing 20 years of service. They thought the one star meant Rear Admiral!

It also led to great support from the friendly natives. One night I took my gorgeous blond, Jackie, who was now a Navy WAVE, to the famous Barney's steak house on Randolph St. We were both in dress whites, and as we stood at the Maitre d's stand, waiting for a table, (apparently a spectacular couple) conversation in this vast dining room gradually dropped to zero. Then applause began and lasted for almost a minute. Dinner was on the house. Wow! What a way to fight a war. Reality would come later. Actually, it came that night.

Jackie told me she had orders to report to Washington We promised over our last long night together to write every day, visit on leaves, and continue our love after the war. But I think we both knew this would be a long war and only our memories would really survive.

I learned to fly and do acrobatics in this beautiful N3N Bi-plane at Naval Air Station, Glenview, and then flew it as a floatplane at NAS Corpus Christi.
PhotoFrom Acclaimed Images

Back at the base, we were learning to fly in a Navy trainer called an N3N. This was an open cockpit bi-plane with a fixed landing gear. The only communication was one-way from the instructor in the front cockpit to the cadet in the rear cockpit through a tube called a "gosport". He had a mirror above his head on the top wing so he could be sure you were still there and hopefully understood his directions.

I was lucky. My instructor, Lt. Bill Moore, turned out to be a great guy. I had no idea what would be involved in our first flight. Of course I was tense, but managed a smile to seem relaxed and confident. At 5000 ft. he said: "I'm going to show you some of the tricks you're going to learn...assuming you don't wash out before you finish." I kept my feet loosely on the rudder petals, and my right hand on the joystick so I would have some feeling for his maneuvers.

Then he proceeded to fly two loops, one "Immelman" (a half loop where you roll over at the top), a "snap roll" (where the plane is jerked around its orbit, going in the same direction) and a "slow roll" (the same end result but done very smoothly), a "stall" where the plane loses all forward speed, then noses down in a "tailspin". For a climax, he pulled back the throttle and simulating an emergency, "side slipped" into a perfect landing at one of the practice fields. I survived, tried to look like I expected this violent check out as routine. He said, "I think you'll probably make It, but Eddy, I'm going to challenge you every step of the way".

Discipline at Glenview was rather casual. It wasn't Annapolis and we weren't Midshipmen. So no one objected when, as a class, we decided to wear the same unwashed khaki pants until we soloed. Our barracks was like a dorm. Every morning at 0600 a Petty Officer would yell, "Rise and shine" or occasionally, "Drop your cocks and grab your socks".

The shower room was immense and we were all on display. One chap was very well endowed and the object of some attention. Enjoying his obvious pre-eminence, one morning he bragged: "when I'm hard I can hold up a wet towel". Bets were placed. He aroused himself, placed the wet towel.. and won the money! Someone muttered it was just a GI towel. Sour grapes!

*   *   *   *   *

After a few hours of dual instruction, Lt. Moore decided I was a reasonable risk to bring back the Navy's pride and joy in one piece. So I took off - alone. It was lunchtime and no one was hanging around but the Chief, Windy Watson, who cranked up the engine. He probably had his fingers crossed for the whole ten minutes it took me to fly twice around the base and build up the courage to try my first solo landing.

It was probably the longest student approach ever made, but finally the ground came up to meet me and I had done it! Windy gave me a bear hug as if I were the first cadet to ever do it. Over three years later I made what I knew would be my last Navy landing in a fighter on the island of Guam. I used virtually the entire mile long runway! You can't be too careful.

At this point, military discipline finally began in the form of a Marine Sargeant / Drill Instructor. It actually felt exciting to execute close order drill, but one of our ranks was rather chubby, always looked a little out of place, and fell behind when we double-timed. The D I picked on him unmercifully. Later, however, when we were about to graduate and paraded in dress blues for the commanding officer, we were a pretty snappy outfit.

Much later, His Chubbiness became a primary instructor and was in the front cockpit when his student climbed into the rear seat for his first flight. Of course you can guess - It was the brutal Marine Sargeant who had transferred into flight training. Our friend looked in the mirror and said into the gosport, "Small world isn't it, Sarge", then proceeded to practically fly the wings off the poor N3N.

* * * * *

Having soloed, we began the next of four more segments. Stick with me as I teach you how to fly an N3N, the Navy way in 1942

This involved learning to handle emergencies and make the safest possible landing in the best available road or field. First things first - lower the nose to keep flying speed. Then look around and try to find a landing site you could safely reach with your current altitude.

If initially you were high enough, you would circle it. In any case, your final approach hopefully had a few hundred feet to spare and you would give this up with an "S" turn approach or a "side-slip" like Lt. Moore had used on my first flight. Then you slowed to a stalling speed a foot or two above the ground and landed. In a real emergency, since you had no radio, you walked home, unless some kind soul offered you a lift.

Moore thought I had this drill under control and I was ready for a "check flight" with another instructor, to get a second opinion on my progress. The "check" instructor pulled the throttle back a few times to simulate engine failure and I managed to make decent approaches using both techniques and got a thumbs "up". So now, on to "acrobatics".

Performing highflying aerial maneuvers was not exactly my favorite activity, but I performed them with reasonable success. Another "check" flight...another "up". Later when I was an instructor at an advanced training squadron, I had to teach cadets how to handle an "outside spin". This was a bitch. You entered it by doing a half loop, then at the top, on your back, instead of finishing the loop, you pushed the nose up and up until the plane lost all flying speed and flipped over for its crazy nose down dive back to earth.

Unlike the classic "tailspin" where you were on the inside of the rotation, you were obviously now on the outside of the spinning plane. The centrifical force was enormous and rather painful with the blood rushing to your head. Only your seat belt kept you from becoming a UFO. This happened to one cadet (not mine) but fortunately his chute opened. The solution was to slowly force your feet back onto the rudder pedals and stop the rotation. Then you somehow managed to grab the basic control stick and gradually pull out of the steep dive! I wonder if this weird maneuver disappeared from the training syllabus after WWII.

Our next stage, D, was "formation flying" in which two cadets would fly solo with an instructor flying a third plane. He would lead, and by hand signals, hold us either close aboard on either side, and slightly behind him. (This was relatively easy.) Or he would change us to a diagonal line of the three planes. In this case the second cadet was trying to hold position on the first cadet, and if this chap was at all unsteady, the variations were magnified for the second cadet - moderate chaos! While we were not exactly the superb Navy jet acrobats - the Blue Angels, most of the folks in nearby Evanston, according to the local newspaper, thought we were magnificent.

But one woman wrote to the paper that we were making too much noise flying low over town. Another answered that we could roll our wheels on her roof, If it would make us better pilots. Civilian support!

During these three months of learning to fly for Navy, there was limited ground school and ample time to swap stories of our civilian days. All the Northwestern guys knew the finale of my favorite tale, but not the unusual build-up.

One of my Phi Gam fraternity brothers was dating a nurse from the Cradle, a home for unwed mothers rented from Northwestern. He said they were three-months overdue on their rent and we had to help them avoid eviction. It was obviously beyond our means, but someone suggested a dance before Thanksgiving break could help. This idea was going nowhere, until Corby Robertson suggested it might work if we had a big name band - and Tommy Dorsey was in Chicago!

So Corby and his beautiful cheerleader and I drove down to the Palmer House. The Maitre d' thought our idea was a very long shot, but gave us a table next to the bandstand and asked Tommy to join us. Tommy, bless his soul, thought it was a brilliant piece of charity. "I can bring maybe five horns and drums. Jo Stafford and the Pied Pipers will come along. But don't count on old Blue Eyes" (Frank Sinatra was his male vocalist!)

We charged $3 per head, filled old Patten Gym, and saved the Cradle.

The check flight at the end of stage D was critical. In effect it was a review of your ability to handle all the challenges you had faced to this point in your training. An "up" virtually guaranteed you would be shipped out to the Naval Air Station (NAS) Corpus Christi for the next level of instruction – Intermediate - in more advanced aircraft. Here, success would lead to your Advanced Squadron, which could be in one of many different planes preparing you for ultimate fleet duty. Finally, a passing grade through all of these flying drills and intense ground school and you were awarded your coveted NAVY WINGS.

Two of my best buddies and I had breezed through the first check flights. Since we were obviously hot pilots, we figured the D check would be easy. So we booked a suite in the Drake Hotel for the Post Check Party and lined up three fun loving girls who would enjoy an overnight celebration I reasoned, rather easily, that Jackie would forgive my unfaithfulness under the circumstances

That morning, Lt. Moore and I had a one-hour warm up flight. Then the check pilot jumped into the front cockpit. When Moore saw who it was, he rolled his eyes and showed me crossed fingers. By the luck of the draw, so to speak, I got the man who was cordially hated by the other instructors since he gave more "downs" than the rest of them combined.

I didn't know this, but I sensed a problem and was just a little nervous. Everything went smoothly until the emergency check. Of six simulated problems, all in difficult situations, I handled five perfectly. In the sixth, I landed safely, but a little too "hot". And the bastard gave me a "down".

To offset the "down" required flying two "ups" in back to back check flights. Moore was furious, and knowing our party plans, arranged for two more flights with other instructors that afternoon. They were friends of his, and knowing the background and probably his opinion of my ability, gave me relatively smooth and easy checks. Both were "ups"...and it was on to the Drake!

There was only one problem. After more than five hours in the air under considerable pressure and strain, I was on borrowed time as a party man. After two drinks and a few dances, I virtually passed out. My room service steak was uneaten. My date said "Romeo...phooey!" And took a taxi home. But I was on my way to Corpus!

With three friends and ample gas ration coupons, we drove to Texas in the dull but dependable two-tone used Dodge my mother gave me as a "graduation" present from Glenview. Later I lucked into a good trade for a 1941 Ford V-8 convertible that became a treasure for the rest of the war.

The Ford V-8 was an icon of its era. The style of our 1941 treasure would still draw admiring glances at a Concourse d'Elegance.

Naval Air Station, Corpus Christi, Texas, was a different world. The easy going days of Glenview and the wild and woolly liberties in Chicago became loving memories. Here everything was snap and polish, strictly by the book. At the main gate the armed guard checked our orders and said I could drive the car in to the cadet headquarters, unload our gear, and bring it back to park forever more in "that there parking lot".

We were billeted eight to a room with one senior cadet as a sort of advisor / monitor. There were frequent and unannounced inspections. Tidiness was next to Godliness and the whole room would be put "on report" and subject to disciplinary action for any loose gear. We found a "mole" in the inspection office and learned when our room would be checked. Then one of us would get a "bed check" from Sick Bay for some imagined illness, and be put under a blanket in an upper bunk. Which was then stuffed with all the gear we didn't know where it should go.

*   *   *   *   *

There were morning and evening formations for the entire cadet corps. One night at the flag lowering ceremony, the regular bugler was sick and the officer-in-charge asked for a volunteer. Being in the front row and a Boy Scout bugler of some skill, I held up my hand, took the proffered bugle and blew "Tattoo", the proper bugle call to lower the flag, like Miles Davis.

The reward was unexpected...shouts and applause from my classmates, and the Officer in charge gave me a weekend pass. I talked him into including two buddies, Dick Hof and Dave Krafthefer. We decided to take my car and drive across the border from Corpus Christi to Monterey, Mexico.

The first night was Margaritas and music in the swinging old town section. High as kites, we heard there was an exotic bordello in a castle on the outskirts of town. We were easy pickings for the pretty hookers. Back at our swishy hotel, the desk clerk said that tomorrow night was a fancy party on the roof garden. Maybe if we looked good we would be invited.

So we put on our fancy Dress Whites. The elegant hostess spotted the three Navy dudes in the lobby and we were cordially invited. They were short of men for this engagement party and we were hot numbers with the young beauties. The roof garden was decorated to the nines. Lanterns swayed in the gentle breeze. Tables were laden with dozens of Mexican specialties, the orchestras played with gusto - cariocas and big band tunes non-stop.

One had a great figure and flashing black eyes. They caught mine. In her colorful whirling skirt and my Navy whites, we were an International sensation that danced till the last horn blew farewell. She asked me if I knew she was the daughter of the Mayor of nearby Nuevo Laredo. What luck! I dated her as often as I could as a cadet back at Corpus. Her father was so pleased with the attention that he gave me half a case of an almost forgotten treasure - Vat 69 Scotch. First time I was paid for something I enjoyed. Gigolo Jorge. Our venue, after a movie or a little local dancing, was the back seat of the now wonderful old Dodge. I was very careful not to create a more living memory.

Also among the guests was the Manager of the local beer company. He invited us to the brewery the next morning. The tasting room was underground, air conditioned, and the different dark beers were fabulous. After two hours we said we must leave and head home to Corpus.

But it was 110 degrees back in the real world and the car was not air-conditioned. Remember, this was 1942. The drive home was the longest, hottest, driest, and slowest in history. We had no water. The car boiled over once. Thank God for the friendly natives. We were treated like Gringo Kings from a foreign land. Body language replaced Spanish, and with water, fruits, candies and neighborly love, we made it back... from the sublime to the pathetic – overnight.

* * * * *

Now began our "Intermediate" syllabus. flown in a low wing aluminum Vultee Vanguard nicknamed the "vibrator". It had a retractable landing gear and a two-speed prop. You wore a helmet with earphones and could communicate with your instructor in the front cockpit. After a relatively short period of indoctrination in the Vanguard, it was on to Instrument training.

Back in Primary training with our bi-plane N3N, the only instruments on our dashboard were the Needle, which measured the degree of angle of our wings to the horizon, and in the same dial, the Ball that showed the amount of skid or sidewise movement. In a smooth bank, they would show neutral. Separately, the Airspeed indicator obviously showed the speed of the plane through the air (not over the ground.), and the altimeter.

In the Vanguard we met the "Artificial Horizon", an amazing device. Sixty years ago this was high-tech for single engine training planes! It would show the plane's relationship to the horizon, both angle of the wings and the up or down angle of the nose. We also still had the good old Needle / Ball unit as a back-up because the Artificial Horizon was not fool-proof, and of course our airspeed indicator and altimeter.

Stay with me…the training becomes more exciting!

Our first chance to fly on instruments was on land, in the Link Trainer, an ingenious machine that simulated the cockpit of a real plane. With the black hood drawn overhead, you were literally in the dark and totally dependent on the instruments to "fly" safely. The Link operator could instruct you to perform all the various maneuvers like take-off, turning, and approach to landing. Once you earned an "up" check in the Link, it was off to the real world of actually flying blind in the Vanguard.

The few hours of dual instruction under the hood included flying the Vanguard in a holding pattern between the airport and a radio "Cone of Silence" about five miles away. You flew outbound on the right side of a straight line. In your earphones you would hear an "A" (dot dash) if you were in the right location, when you no longer heard the signal, you were obviously at the cone of silence. You turned 180 degrees and flew back to the main station on the left side hearing an "N" (dash dot) if you were right on. In all this you would try to maintain a steady altitude and airspeed.

After satisfying my instructor that I was safe to solo (blind!) although he was always in the plane, I found myself once again on the accursed "check" flight. My check pilot was a seasoned vet from active duty with the fleet. His smile reassured me that I would get a fair review. Little did I know, until later, that once again I had drawn the toughest cookie, and that his smile was the result of surgery on his face to correct the result of a crash landing. He was extremely demanding and required me to fly the holding pattern twice, and virtually land on instruments, which I had never practiced.

It was a long flight. When we got out of the plane he said two words: "Nice work" and gave me the high five! Months later his rigorous style probably saved my life.

This workhorse helped train pilots for the Navy and Air Force, as well as our allies for over 20 years. I instructed in this plane and flew it from Kingsville to Wichita to court Kay.
Picture of a restored SNJ, courtesy of Brian Lockett

In this event, as an officer, I was on an "Overnight Training Flight", in a more advanced training plane called an SN-J, I was on my way to Wichita for a romantic rendezvous. I had to stop at the Air Corps base in Dallas for fuel. It had been cloudless when, with another instructor as co-pilot, I took off from Corpus. At Dallas the ceiling was 500' and we were rather suddenly in the clouds and flying on instruments. The first time since the check flight as a student.

I reported my position to the Control Tower and they said "NAVY 203 - hold at 5000 feet until instructed" So it was out to the Cone of Silence on the right side and back to the airport on the left side...five times! In these conditions planes were surely stacked up around Dallas. It was a new ball game for me. I had no idea if there were others near my assigned altitude, but I was trying to be very careful. Finally the Tower said, "NAVY 203 descend to 2000 feet and continue to hold". Of course I was sweating blood and not sure how long I could keep my cool. So I told the Tower I was short on fuel and. after an agonizing wait, they said "OK NAVY.. You're clear or land"

But by then I had lost some of my concentration and practically flew into the ground at much too fast an airspeed - almost 100 knots over the maximum recommended for this plane - in a "deadly spiral". Happily I broke out of the overcast at 300 feet about a mile from the runway and landed safely. Whew.

My original flight plan showed Wichita as the final destination, but because of the weather I had to file another flight plan and get approval to continue. The Air Force Major in charge said: "You had really tough conditions coming in here, Ensign...sure you want to go on?" "Yes Sir", I said, still shaking inside, "it was pretty much routine". After all, I had the reputation of the U.S. NAVY to uphold!.

So, after refueling, we were cleared for Wichita. That segment had a few thrills of its own, but I'm saving those for the chapter on my creative courtship of Kathryn Jane which had started in Wichita two months previously.

*   *   *   *   *

to the training experience. Having completed Intermediate, it was on to Advanced and hopefully our Navy wings. Three basic programs were offered; big twin-engine flying boats, single engine trainers that would lead to operational fighters and dive or torpedo bombers, and single engine float planes. We were given our choice. Ha.

Almost everyone wanted "fighters" except a few who thought the multi-engine experience could lead to airliners after the war. But you got whatever the brass assigned. This was influenced by the projected needs of the fleet and the capacity of the base to comply. The least popular, by far, was the single engine float planes. That's what I got. Actually, they were kind of fun!

There were two models... our old friend the so-called "yellow peril" N3N bi-plane and the operational fleet plane, the OS2U. Both had the single main float (think "pontoon") secured directly under the fuselage, and a small float attached near the end of each wing. The OS2U was a low wing aluminum design with a machine gun mounted behind the rear cockpit for the radioman / gunner in actual fleet use, but used by the instructor for dual instruction.

As cadets, we began in the N3N. The venue was a protected harbor adjoining the main base near the Officer's Club. Rather quickly we learned how to taxi safely on water, allowing for the effect of wind and waves, and return to the main launching area for pick up by crane. Take-offs were also easy, but landings required a little practice to judge your height above the water when it was smooth and / or there was no easy horizon to help. We also flew at night, which increased the variables for safe landings.

One day on the way to ground school, a dog joined my footsteps. He was non-descript but had a warm and laughing face. When I stopped, he stopped. Clearly I had a new friend. This was "Drift Angle". A cadet dog with a history of attachments. It was my turn.

For two weeks we were inseparable and I loved this dog. Until a substitute instructor in ground school was repeating the same course we'd had the day before on how to quickly recognize Jap bombers. I wasn't sure it was the same course. Drift Angle knew it was. He looked at me and when I didn't move. He stood up and left the room. Sadly, that was the end of this tour of Drift Angle duty.

As cadets, fitness was an important part of our lives. Most of the Phys / Ed guys were great athletes and we tried to play the part. But one Ensign was a real prick. After a tough workout he would have us double time around the 440 track- sometimes twice. We damn near died and vowed we'd get even.

Well, one day the instructors challenged us to a touch football game - aha! I was a good punter and was included as right end on our 7-man team. Rules for touch vary widely. This time, blocking was allowed. Like that wonderful sequence in the TV show MASH when the other team had a fabulous "scat back" and Alan Alda's team gave him a little secret injection (I'll always remember that, as doctors, they also swabbed his arm before the needle!), We waited for the right moment for revenge.

It came when our leader called for a run around my end. I could see the villain watching the ball carrier and I rolled into his thighs with my every ounce - just as our left end sailed into his shoulders. The perfect "high / low". They carried him off. End of game. End of double-time.

*   *   *   *   *

About a year later, when I was assigned to this same squadron as instructor, I spent three weeks flying night instructions in the N3N. This was disciplinary action for being a day late from leave.   As a sort of extra punishment...my students were "lend / lease" officers from our South American allies. These high-ranking officers presumably were capable pilots who requested seaplane training from our government. They got me - at night. Or rather I got them. Throw in the language barrier and it was pretty spooky.

Remember the one-way "gosport" tube from the instructor in the front cockpit, now me, to Senor Major or Colonel in the student seat. I would explain in simple language how our time would be spent - taxiing, touch and go landings, and a brief flight over the Gulf and home to our beloved crane (then off to the Officer's Club for a much needed Jack Daniels.) I would ask, "Do you understand me, senor?" and they would always smile and nod "Si! Si!"

I would make the first landing and ask them to follow me through on the controls. Then it would be their turn. Oops! Almost invariably we would have nosed into the drink if I didn't overpower the controls. And so for almost a month, none of my really very nice students made a solo landing. But we all lived through it.

Back to flying as a cadet, an "up" in the N3N led to more sophisticated operations in the OS2U. This plane was virtually outmoded by the time I learned to fly it. The OS2U mission in the fleet was to be the eyes of Battleships and Cruisers. Launched from catapults, it would observe and direct the big ships bombardments, maybe spot an enemy sub, and deliver personnel.

To provide a smooth sea for safe landing, the mother ship would have to turn 90 degrees to the wind, for what was called a "cast recovery", then lower a crane to pick up the plane after it taxied alongside. Not a popular maneuver for the ship's commander. Not a popular role for the pilot. A friend of mine from Glenvue days, Phil Schaack, served as one and said he always drew duty as a watch captain when his ship was in port! The other officers objected to his getting "flight pay" (an extra 50%) for rather infrequent flights. With more carrier task forces, these planes were used less and less.

One distinct element to the OS2U training syllabus was the catapult shot. I had two as a cadet and a few more as an instructor. As the name implies, this is sort of a slingshot. The plane is hoisted onto a narrow metal ramp. When the charge of compressed air is "fired", the plane is propelled up to flying speed and you're airborne. Again, this experience saved my life one night on a carrier in the Pacific.

Finally, in March 1943, after eight months of blood and sweat, tears and laughs, I graduated as an Officer and a Gentleman from NAS Corpus Christi. This Certificate to Ensign George A. Eddy as a Naval Aviator shows the OS2U, the plane with the float, that I flew in advanced training.

Naval Air Training Center

United States Naval Air Station
Corpus Christi, Texas

Know all men by these presents that

Ensign George A. Eddy, A-V(N), USNR

has completed the prescribed course of training and having met successfully the requirements of the course has been designated a

Naval Aviator

In Witness Whereof, this certificate has been signed on this 3rd day of March 1943 and the Seal of the Naval Air Station hereunto affixed

NAVAL AVIATOR'S Graduation Certificate. Floatplane shown at the top is OS2U flown as student and instructor.

More on the "blood" later in a freak accident on land. By chance I was. commissioned an Ensign in the Naval Reserve. By chance, because The Navy Department wanted an equal number of Marine 2nd Lieutenants.

Strangely, at a big meeting of the graduates, where we were seated alphabetically, we're told that those in even number seats would be designated Marines. I was odd, so to speak. My buddies on either side ended the war as Majors, I just made full Lieutenant. It did make a difference for them - pay and prestige! The Marine Corps has a very special and well-deserved spirit. But in the end, there was an offset...I was a member of the elite... a carrier pilot! I was proud of my Navy Wings. And still wear them on Veterans Day.

George H. W. Bush Sr., our 41st President,.certainly earned his wings as a torpedo plane pilot (not a fighter pilot as he is called in most TV shows) who was shot down in the Pacific. I think his son, George W. Bush, President number 43, was wearing Navy Wings on his flight jacket when he was landed on the deck of the Abraham Lincoln. You remember the carrier was staged off San Diego for that dismal "Mission Accomplished" photo-op from the Iraq war. Maybe, instead, he should have worn his wings from limited service during the Viet Nam war - in the Texas Air National Guard.

*　　*　　*　　*　　*

After graduation, my orders were to remain at Corpus as an instructor in the "float" squadron from which I had graduated with honor. While eager to get to the fleet and help win the war, this wasn't bad duty. First of all, it was on the main station, instead of one of the several outlying fields. The BOQ's (Bachelor Officer's Quarters) were quite decent. The "O" club was fancy with frequent

Corpus were fun and games for the excitement of the moment.

Virtually the only subjects officers talked about were flying and women…a little time was allowed for the war, and booze. We were allowed to buy two bottles per month. I chose Schenley Black Label "bourbon" (which we called Black Death, It was 50% grain neutral spirits) because I had known the CEO, Louis Rosensteil in Florida. His son, David, and I were good friends at age 12. We would go out on their 50' mahogany fishing boat used to entertain Schenley distributors. David and I would play the billfish up to the boat, then the guests would land them for the photo op.

A BOQ neighbor from Nashville told me to stop buying this awful hooch, and get straight Tennessee bourbon. So I switched to the other option, what is now the popular national brand – Jack Daniels!

Months later, when my friend Ted and I were both flying in San Diego, I ran into an old golf competitor from prep school days, Frank Beacham, who was dating a very attractive brunette, Maudie Fellowes. Her father had been a Marine Major. This is the girl for Ted, I think, and sure enough their courtship eventually grew into marriage and we all became friends again after the war.

NAS Corpus was a magnet for celebrities. Bob Hope, with his beautiful girl friends and live swing band, came to call and was cheered with wild abandon. Then one day FDR came to visit. It probably took 5 minutes for the entire air base to hear the exciting news…THE PRESIDENT IS HERE.!!!

Of course it was the worst possible flying weather. Low

scuddy clouds, 30 knot winds. Corpus Bay looked like a tsunami had hit. We instructors were told - get every plane in the air – but no cadets. I was assigned an N3N to fly "touch and go" landings in the Bay. It was survival of the fittest. I found out that it is really true - every seventh wave is smoother. I did my duty and finally flew back to base.

My landing pattern was over the O club. I could see that the President was in the rear seat of an open convertible. I rocked my wings and waved. I flew for FDR!

The word passed that the President had said: "it must be very hard to fly out there". The Admiral reputedly said: "Mr. President, it is challenging, Sir, but that's what those cadets are here to learn."

*   *   *   *   *

Now my life was going to change 180 degrees. It was on return to base, from my second leave as an officer, that I met Kathryn Jane Corbett.

My flight from Chicago stopped first in Kansas City. No problem. Then another stop in Wichita. Big problem. It was about 3 AM when the Braniff DC-3 taxied to the terminal. The door was opened; the ladder lowered, and up came this drop dead beautiful creature. "Will Ensign Eddy please hold up his hand?" Which I did, not having any idea what was to follow. "Sorry, sir, we need your seat for a priority passenger. You can pick up your bag in the terminal."

All of my protests about being late from leave, courts martial, brig, and on and on were futile. I left the plane as my Air Force seatmate said, "Go get her, Navy!" The DC-3 left for Corpus without me. At least the coffee shop was open and I invited "Kay" to join me... turning a lemon into a lemonade as the saying goes. We were rather quickly simpatico and talked for at least an hour.

Then she called the Allis Hotel and booked me a room, ordered a taxi, and I gave her a ride home. That would have been the end of a brief encounter, except the phone in my hotel room suddenly rang and a sweet voice said: "I just wanted to make sure everything was OK". Wow! Instead it became the start of what must be considered one of the most unusual courtships of WWII

The next morning, it was back to the Airport. No seats on Braniff or TWA for at least three days and then standby. So I would have to figure out a train or bus alternative. In Navy blues with gold wings I was a visible - and obviously unhappy person. That's when an Air Force Major said: "You look like you've lost your best friend - what's up?" I explained my problem and he said: "Well, we have a DC-3 and we're flying to Texas. Our base is about 80 miles from Corpus, and you're welcome to come along".

There were four majors and a sargeant radioman. They had been hunting in South Dakota and the plane was loaded with pheasants. They were also inveterate bridge players and eager to resume their game. After takeoff I was asked if I had ever flown twin engine. I said no. " Well come up to the cockpit", said the head major, John Hughes, "and I'll show you how".

The bridge game started and with the sarge navigating, I flew the Air Force brass home. When we were close to their field, I prepared to give up my pilot's seat but my new instructor said "Sit still, I'll talk you through the landing." Smooth as silk. As a bonus, I was given the 80-mile ride to my Navy base in Major Hughes' jeep, and two pheasants!

Now the challenge was to get back to Wichita to woo my suddenly beloved. Since I had been AOL (Absent Over Leave), I was not likely to get another leave for at least six months, besides having to tutor the South American officers at night. as punishment.

*   *   *   *   *

What to do? We had quickly established that her father would not let her fly down here, into a presumed nest of scoundrels, even free on Braniff. By chance, I heard that the Navy allowed occasional overnight training hops, but the catch was a limit of 700 miles. The main base where I was stationed was about 750 miles. One of the other bases, Kingsville, was 680 miles. Through networking at the O club, I met the Lt. Cmdr. in charge of the advanced fighter squadron stationed at Kingsville.

"Sir", I said, "I want to get to the fleet, and not in these

OS2Us. I know I will be a good fighter pilot and you can check that I am an excellent instructor." Well, he did, and when he had an opening, I got it. Naturally, as the new boy, I had to log quite a few hours (including teaching "inverted spin" recoveries) before I could even approach the overnight flight event. As it turned out, this was not overly popular, and after two months, I applied and got the OK.

The instrument approach and my stop in Dallas, as I covered earlier, led on to the final leg to Wichita. With my friend, Don Leahy, in the back seat navigating, we reported to the Wichita control tower, expecting instrument approach instructions. But the response was: "Navy 203, you are cleared to land VFR (visual flight rules)".

Hey wait a minute! We were over solid clouds at 3000 feet. I asked Don on the intercom, "Where the hell do you think we are" He said he thought we were right on our flight plan. We agreed to bluff it out, get down to the ground (a little more safely than at Dallas) and find some landmarks -. "Roger, tower, from Navy 203"!

At about 500 feet we broke out of the clouds.... right over a railroad track. Navigation was now simple. Follow the tracks to the first station! Happily it was nearby and the town was on our map. We turned back about 20 miles and there was the big beautiful Wichita airport.

Kay and a nifty friend for Don came out to meet us. The next day we called Kingsville, "The weather is so bad here in Kansas,

Skipper, it's a regular Blue Norther! We'll try to fly home tomorrow" And tomorrow and tomorrow! Our improbable love was still warm and wonderful. As I bring back these memories, I realize we knew so little about each other, even with our long letters and phone calls. Later she would become a successful artist and a leader in the world of american craft, I would prosper in business, and we would raise a wonderful family. All I knew then was that she should be with me always.

After dancing and romancing at the Blue Moon, I took her home. At the door, in my arms, I asked her to marry me. The answer was immediate - a long loving kiss. Kay's mother was ecstatic. Her father was highly skeptical. I said I'd be back with the ring as soon as possible, actually having no idea when it would be.

*　*　*　*　*

So back to Kingsville and now a covert mission for Ensign Eddy - how to return to Wichita. A little research disclosed that the twin-engine trainers used at Corpus were made at the factory of Beech Aircraft…in Wichita, and the need for them was expanding. Light bulb lights! I'll volunteer to ferry one from the plant to the base. Two problems: I wasn't a twin-engine pilot (The Army DC-3 time would hardly count) and there were dozens of qualified officers already in line.

Getting checked out wasn't too difficult. An old fraternity brother, Bob Horder, who owed me a big one, was teaching in twin Beeches at the main station. He took me up every chance we were both free and In about six weeks I had the 12 hours required to qualify.

Just who made the trip, it turns out, was entirely at the discretion of a Chief Petty Officer... in the WAVES! A charming lady who enjoyed going drinking and dancing with a wannabe Fred Astaire. So as not to chill this romance, I commented one night that I had family in Wichita that I hadn't seen for some time and maybe one day I could ferry a Beech back to Corpus. Since she was stationed on the main base, and I was now at Kingsville, it wasn't easy to apply my most loving technique. But with a few rum and cokes and rumbas we worked out the logistics, and I got the assignment.

Ah, the sordid machinations of true love.

The twin-engine trainer was built in Wichita, Kay's hometown. I learned to fly it so I could ferry one back to NAS Corpus, and romance my love before taking off.
Photo from Tom Philo, www taphilo.com

The Beech plant was chockablock with women. Each was known as 'Rosie the Riveter'. A friend of Kay's family was in charge of PR and said he'd be grateful if he could tour me through the plant, to kind of show off who was flying the planes they were working on twelve hours a day. Well, I'm not exactly Clark Gable but in the Naval Aviator's green uniform with a sun tan and blond crew cut...production stopped for about a half hour! There was lots of "Hey man! I'll give you a home cooked dinner – for starters" and some even more exciting offers.

The next day, with a radioman that had come up with me, we checked out our assigned plane and taxied to the end of the one runway. Half the plant had come out to watch their new hero take-off. I took one look at the one runway and thought...Oh God! It was about the width of an alley, with several minor hills and valleys. The wind was about 25 knots, and blowing directly across the runway from the right.

My 12 or so hours of twin-engine practice had not included a crosswind takeoff, so I had to create an instant strategy. Well. the plane has manually operated wing flaps, mainly to slow it down for landing, but they could give us extra lift for a faster take-off. I told the radioman to stand by to crank them down like crazy when I gave the signal.

This plane has an old-fashioned landing gear design...it sits " nose up" over the two main wheels and the tail is down on a small tail wheel. I pushed the throttles to virtually full power and when the tail came up to a horizontal position I released the brakes. We began to roar down the runway, and I lifted the left wing slightly to compensate for the crosswind. "Crank", I yelled. He did and we sort of floated into the air. It was a long runway and by the time we were over our waving fans, I had the flaps and the wheels up, and we rocked our wings and goosed the engines.

There had been only one problem with the trip. The engagement ring my mother had picked out for me and sent to Kingsville had the jewelers name on the rather obvious package and was swiped from the mail room. I explained, but Kay's father was not convinced. Later a replacement made the scene, the day before the ceremony!!

I flew Braniff back to Wichita a month later, and suddenly, I was a married man... after a total of six dates with my bride. But in wartime with raging hormones, perhaps this was not so unusual. Four of my best friends flew a Beech up from Corpus for the wedding. The night before, with dates, we celebrated at the Blue Moon with 3.2 beer spiked with "imported" Jack Daniels, and Vaughn Monroe belting out his signature song, "Racing with the moon".

The ceremony was pre-war, with proper pomp and circumstance in the Presbyterian Chapel. Kay wore the same wedding dress that my mother and sister had worn.

*   *   *   *   *

I finally did go to the fleet, as a Fighter / Bomber pilot aboard the carrier INTREPID, now a marvelous museum on the Hudson River in New York City. My plane was the gull-winged F4U CORSAIR, made famous by the Marine Ace, Col. Pappy Boyington, who shot down more Jap Zeros than any other U.S. pilot. It was a powerful beast, exciting to fly.

My last "landing" on the INTREPID was with three grandchildren. When they saw the fabulous film of flight deck operations, one said; "Gee, Gramps, did you do THAT?" It was over 60 years ago, but the juices flowed and I knew I could do it again…probably easier in a jet than in my wonderful old prop plane!

My first carrier landing was quite an event. That comes after the Honeymoon and early-married life in Texas. Hang on.

* * * * *

We headed for a honeymoon in Chicago... at the elegant Drake Hotel of course! As the Braniff flight approached Kansas City for an interim stop, one of the Stews said, "I'm really sorry, but I have some bad news...we can only give you one seat from KC to Chicago." Tears formed in Kay's eyes. I said we' d both get off. Then the Captain came back with a huge grin and said "Just a little company joke!"

The honeymoon was fabulous, compared to my other affairs. There were family parties and box seats for OKLAHOMA! But just three days, and we were back at Corpus. I took a suite at the Robert Driscoll Hotel to ease my bride into Texas and Navy life. I would commute each night from Kingsville and the pad was always filled with good ole boys and my sweetie and my booze. After five days I ran out of money and it was time to face married life at an outlying field.

There were no Married Officer's Quarters available for us, so I was forced to scrounge around and the best available was a kind of motel with a small kitchen / living room, and tiny bedroom. When I carried Kay over the threshold, she cried - not in happiness, but in realization that this would be our "home" for the foreseeable future.

Actually, it wasn't all that bad. There was a half-ass O club, many young married officers and wives, frequent bar-b-cue parties, occasional flicks. And we had each other.

* * * * *

.Would be fighter pilots, like me, dreamed of going to the fleet to help personally win the war. That really meant flying off aircraft carriers day and night, which was both exciting, and a little scary, when you remembered you were going to land on the small deck of a big ship rolling in the high seas.

Finally, it was my chance. I was ordered first to Photo School, in Pensacola, for four months of land and aerial photography. This was kind of a kick. NAS Pensacola was an older base and very elegant, with a golf course and sailboats to borrow. Kay and I rented a little house and bought a Cocker Spaniel that Kay named Gypsy.

KAY, the author, and GYPSY in Pensacola.

My first month was using a Graphlex camera, now a museum piece. The second month was the standard news camera of the day, the Speed Graphic. Both used 4x5 negatives. My Minolta today fits in my shirt pocket. Month three, we shot movies, Our instructor was Leif Erickson (I'm not sure of the spelling), a B player in Hollywood who regaled us with dozens of secrets about reigning stars. Month four we started on aerial work, in which we would shoot stills and movies from the rear cockpits of various training planes..

When I graduated from Photo School, I was given two sets of orders by the Executive Officer, which was quite unusual. One was sealed, to be opened only by the Commanding Officer, NAS North Island, San Diego - if I made it that far, The Exec said,: "I understand you have been selected to map Japan in a highly modified F4U. A new super-charger will give superior performance at high altitude. You will have three fixed telephoto cameras, the cockpit will be armored. There will be no machine guns. This is top secret, but I thought you should know what extra odds you now would face - just in case. Good Luck!"

*   *   *   *   *

The other orders were transparent - First to NAS Jacksonville for Operational Training in the F4U Corsair, then a special aerial photography school in New Cumberland PA, and carrier checkout in Glenview where I had started my flying career.

So on to Jacksonville. As a city, "Jax" had surprising charm. Great sight lines of the river, harbor, and ocean. A wonderful beach community. Our rented house was pre-fab, pre-war, probably the First World War. If you slammed the front door, the house would shimmy. So of course the third night onboard we had a hurricane – category two! We had no disaster plan, no idea of what to do, stay or seek safety, and no sense of where to go. We decided to tough it out. We put towels and sheets across the windows and doors, and moved furniture for a little more security.

Suddenly the phone rang. It was my new instructor, George Sell, calling during the "eye" of the storm. "We're around the corner, a bunch of us are playing Backgammon, come on over." It was a nice way to survive and make some new friends. The morning after was calm. It was back to the base to resume the drill.

The first of many challenges with this plane was to fly it safely! Quite a huge step up in power from what I had been used to as a student and instructor at Corpus Christi. This machine was the most powerful Navy fighter. It could do over 400 mph which was Godspeed in those days. Then, if needed, for fifteen minutes, you could inject water into the engine for another 25 mph.

My first take-off followed a rather brief cockpit checkout by my instructor, George Sell. I was in the cockpit, and he was leaning in from the side and pointing out what control did what, assuming I knew a hell of a lot more about the Corsair from the printed handbook than I did.

"OK" he said. "Remember, you have to taxi from side to side as you can't see dead ahead with the big nose. Landing is a cinch but don't make a long approach for the same problem -

visibility. Oh yes, there is huge 'torque' when you power up for take off. The plane will run way off to the left if you don't lean on that right rudder. Good luck" (The Corsair was known as the "Ensign Eliminator" because of the vicious torque!)

Good God! What am I doing here in this strange and forbidding cockpit, with all these new gadgets and four times the horsepower I have ever flown? I tell myself I'm here because I'm supposed to be a hot pilot. Well, give it the juice, pray, and get this machine in the air. Suddenly I'm airborne, everything is right with the world, and I'm in heaven. This is MY PLANE! Landing was a cinch.

My wonderful plane from NAS Jacksonville through fleet duty with squadron VBF-14 on the Aircraft Carrier INTREPID, Photo from a WWII war bond poster.

Training included dog fights with the instructor, high altitude flights with oxygen, simulated strafing and bombing runs, night flights and practice carrier landings.

These were on dry land, using a runway marked off the size of a carrier deck. At the incoming corner on the left side, the Landing Signal Officer was stationed. (The Navy made left turns in practice because that's how you approached the ships at sea)

With a highly visible flag in each hand, the LSO would coach you in for a safe landing. If you were too high, the flags would be over his head. If you were going too slow, he would rush the flags from in front of him to each side in a sweeping motion, if you were right on he would hold his arms out straight to the side.

Then he would sweep one hand across his neck as a "cut". You would cut the power, take back control, as it were, and land. If you weren't "in the groove" at the final moment you would get the "wave off" to jam on the power and go around again. I did this drill, day and night, about 20 times until it was second nature. I suspect that today's jets are brought aboard with high-tech instrument LSOs.

The two months in the Navy's special aerial photography school in New Cumberland, PA, were routine, none of the fancy drills I had expected for my future duty. From there it was back to NAS Glenview where I started my cadet training in the early summer of 1942. Kay and I drove our little Ford convertible on the Pennsylvania Turnpike for hours with a broken heater and the temperature 14 degrees below zero

We wore all the coats we owned, and drank hot coffee at every single stop to warm up. A little sense of humor and a lot of love were helpful

*　　*　　*　　*　　*

NAS Glenview was quite different from when I had been an Aviation Cadet in 1942. Now it was home base for carrier checkout on the good ship WOLVERINE and sister ship SABLE. They were Lake Michigan cruise ships before the war, coal-burning paddle wheelers, then modified by the Navy to become small aircraft carriers.

We were slated for a one-day program with practice on land, like Jacksonville, then out to one of the ships if we qualified. It was a miserable day in November, 1944…300' Ceiling, dark gray clouds, and 25 knot winds. In a way, this was good news, because the limited 20 knot maximum speed of these carriers made strong true winds across the deck - a necessity to use the big 4FU fighter, Otherwise, it would have been modified SNJ trainers, which wouldn't count the same in your log book.

My performance in practice was disastrous! The Signal Officer, who turned out to be an old friend of mine, said: "I should flunk you!". I said: "I don't know what went wrong…I can do this in my sleep. Please give me an UP". He grudgingly said: "OK, cause we're friends, but for Christ' sake - don't fuck up! I don't want you in the drink and your soul on my conscience!"

That afternoon, for the first time in my career, I was sick... in the cockpit. The mechanic jumped up on the wing and asked, "Are you OK, Sir?" I lied: "it was just bad soup at lunch". So now was the moment of truth.

The WOLVERINE

A Lake Michigan cruise ship, modified by the Navy to become an aircraft carrier. With sister ship, SABLE, it trained almost 18,000 pilots in landings and take-offs.
Photo by Joe Radigan, MACM USN Retired.

As a Lt. Junior Grade, I was to lead a flight of four Ensigns out to the WOLVERINE. We rendezvoused over the Bahai' Temple on the shore of Lake Michigan, in Wilmette, and headed out to the ship.

I peeled off the formation, and with my heart in my mouth, headed downwind towards the carrier, I was about a hundred feet off the water, and maybe a hundred yards to the side when

I turned towards the stern of the WOLVERINE.

My wheels and flaps and arresting hook were down. I was rock steady at the approach speed of 80 knots and in the groove. The LSO was ready for my approach. His arms were out straight and stayed there for a million moments… until I got the "cut".

The arresting hook caught the first (of 8) wires designed to stop the plane. Perfect!

I took off and came around again and again until I had made the required eight landings. This time I was held on deck. The Captain of the WOLVERINE was on the loud speaker: "Now hear this! Lieutenant Eddy is the first pilot to make eight perfect landings in the history of this ship". The crew cheered! And I flew home on Cloud 9. All of my Ensigns eventually made the team, but I was the hero of the day back at Glenview, especially after my dismal morning warm-up, where the good news beat me home.

I'm sure that in time more pilots made eight landings without a wave-off. In all, almost 18,000 pilots did qualify on either the WOLVERINE or SABLE, but not so many of those flew F4Us. This plane was not used for carrier operation until late in the war and, as noted earlier, it required at least 15 knots of true wind to create enough apparent wind across the decks of these relatively slow paddle wheelers, and Lake Michigan's winds were generally modest.

*   *   *   *   *

With 8 landings on the Lake Michigan carrier WOLVERINE and 100 F4U hours in my logbook, Kay and I took off for San Diego in our perky '41 Ford V8. In my pocket were the sealed orders, but I knew what they were. Remember that I was to map Japan in a special high-altitude F4U. Kay didn't know that our future held this unknown variable.

When I checked in at Naval Aviation Pacific Headquarters, I had no idea what special training lay ahead. Not to worry. The Commander opened and reviewed my sealed orders, carefully paged through my log book, then paused briefly and said: "I'm assigning you to a new F4U fighter / bomber squadron forming down the coast in Chula Vista."

"But Sir", I said: "My orders are very specific" "Fuck those orders", he said, "We need F4U pilots in the fleet. Report to VBF-14 tomorrow". End of conversation. I was bummed – my chance to be a hero was ended, but the offset was extra time ashore with Kay.

Next to the city of San Diego was Coronado Island. Here was the main Naval Aviation headquarters, North Island. And here is where virtually all pilots lived. Just where exactly in this overcrowded island, another couple would find a home was a huge challenge. There was a helpful office, which directed us to the home of a retired Navy Captain. He and his wife helped out by renting one bedroom and bath, with kitchen privileges. Marvelous people and two pets.

One was a trained duck, very bright, like the talented AFLAC duck on TV commercials. It must have been a female. She loved me from the start, but would bite Kay at the first opportunity. So we were careful. The other pet was a huge black cat. We were asked to leave our bedroom window open at night, as the cat would come and go. The first night, about 3 AM I felt this thump on my belly and awoke to a pair of green eyes about an inch from mine - like that night in Corpus! After a moment of terror, the cat nuzzled my nose and we became the best of friends.

Our next move was to an 8-bedroom villa. The downside was, each couple only got a small spot in the fridge. The upside was, the parties were constant! There was a maid which we all shared, at least most of her services. She was also a hooker on the side. And her Johns would snitch our booze

Finally, always trying to improve our digs, we shared a wonderful house with another couple for the rest of our tour of duty in the states.

*   *   *   *   *

The skipper of VBF-14 was Lt. Cmdr Arthur Downing. This would be his third tour with the fleet. He had already been awarded three Navy Crosses! I figured I was in good company. His first two tours were on the USS YORKTOWN. The first Navy

Cross was for action off New Guinea on March 10, 1942, when in spite of heavy anti-aircraft fire, he flew in low and scored a direct hit on a Jap aircraft tender. The second cross was for two bomb hits in spite of heavy fire and Jap zeros that helped sink an enemy carrier in the significant battle of the Coral Sea.

His second tour with the fleet was on the USS WASP. Off the Philippine Islands he was awarded his third Navy Cross for leading a dive bombing attack that damaged and stopped another Jap carrier, and allowed the torpedo planes that followed to sink it, On his return to the WASP, for good measure, he shot down a Zero who, strangely, was trying to land on his carrier. The Jap dropped in the sea and Downing flew in for a routine landing.

Then later he was responsible for the heroic rescue of his wingman, Moose Amundson. who was shot down in action off Okinawa (I think it was Okinawa). He landed safely in the ocean, struggled into his little yellow life raft, and was drifting rapidly towards the enemy coastline. There was a US submarine on station for "air / sea rescue". The sub commander refused Art's plea to move in and pick up Moose. Too close to Jap guns, he said on the radio.

According to some fellow pilots, Art said, "Go in and get my wingman and I'll keep the shore batteries busy", which he did. Others said Art threatened to machine gun the sub's conning tower!. Anyway, the sub went in at periscope depth and Moose hung on till they were safely out of range. Moose spent three weeks on the sub, became a Watch Officer and a popular member of the crew.

*   *   *   *   *

You would logically think that his incredible experiences at sea would have left a mark on Art's shore side personality, but far from it. Art's style was warm and easy. Besides being a hell of a pilot, he was a party boy, and realizing we would shortly be on a fighting ship, we had many parties. One was at another couple's rented house. This one had a fabulous library, well stocked with erotic stories, which we all shared. And I read another amusing book on learning to be a Naval Aviator called "Love at First Flight" by Chuck Spaulding. He had also been a student at The Hill prep school I attended, but two years ahead of me. Maybe Spaulding's book was the hidden germ of this memoir…

In between parties, we would hit the glamorous Officer's Club at the Del Coronado. The historic and magnificent hotel was converted into officer's quarters (and after the war, restored to its storied style). Brandy Alexanders after dinner were standard for Kay and me. If we were ever "over served", I could inhale the helpful oxygen provided in the cockpit before taking off the next morning.

Our training was two months of more dogfights, night flights, aerial gunnery, bombing runs and carrier landings. In dogfights, both pilots would both climb to 10,000', then one pilot would go another 1000' and the game was on. Over and into clouds, climb and dive, speed up and slow down, twist and turn. Finally one pilot got on the other's tail and won the duel. This was exhilarating – maybe the most fun in training for the fleet!

On gunnery practice we would fire two of the four .50 caliber machine guns, mounted in our wings. The target was a long plastic sleeve towed by another plane. Each plane's bullets were painted a different color so we could inspect the sleeve and count our hits after the flight. I figured I won most of these turkey shoots. Often I wondered how I would feel if a Jap Zero were in my sights when I pressed the button to fire. Probably-"take that you bastard"

But bombing runs were not my specialty. These "fighter / bomber" F4Us had "dive brakes" that could slow our speed. We would start about 15,000 feet, on oxygen, then peel off for our dive at about 80 degrees, release our "bomb" at maybe 2000 feet and pull out above the water at 1000 feet. The gravity strain would almost black us out. Our practice bombs were dummy one-pounders. In the strain of the steep dive, I was never sure how much I should "lead" the sled target. I almost hit the towboat itself twice. I guess they didn't get my number!

Art knew of my special photo training, and appointed me Photographic Officer. This was for mostly "point and shoot" assignments, but the Photo Chief and I invented a fixed movie camera, mounted in the belly of the F4U, that would film 20 seconds automatically when the pilot pressed the control to drop his bomb, and record the results as the plane pulled out of his run. This prototype made it up the chain of command and was pronounced "promising" in Washington, but the war had moved too far to warrant production.

One day my wingman, Jimmie Smith, called on the radio that his engine had conked out. With advice from all of us in the air with him, he tried every procedure to get it running again. No luck. We were near the desert and I told him to bail out. He said he'd rather try to land. It was his call. I followed him down and I swear he put that plane, wheels up, in the only level patch in the entire desert. He was rescued by locals and was naturally the toast of the O club.

Not everyone was so skillful or lucky. Training for combat produced its share of casualties. Our squadron lost four pilots. Each was difficult for me to handle, but one was tragic. We lost Moose in a mid-air collision. The other pilot survived. As you may recall, Moose had been shot down on his previous tour, and been rescued by the US sub. He and his wife Sandy were close friends of Kay's and mine. This was the first death I had experienced that made the price of the nasty Japanese war very personal.

Our first squadron carrier drill was three days aboard the light carrier (CVL) Matanikau. Dark clouds and sheets of rain. The Pacific was not cooperating either. Seas were enormous. On take-offs, the bow would go at least 5 feet under and water would flow back across the entire deck. The signal officer would time his "go" signal to when the bow was starting to rise. Pretty tricky. It amazes me now to think what us kids were able to finesse. Landings were a little easier and eventually we all survived and headed back to San Diego to warm beds and cozy wives and girlfriends.

One of our squadron's wives, Betty Westfeldt, wrote a parody to Bob Hope's famous "Thanks for the Memory". The first verse was..."Thanks for the Memory - of a ship the Matanikau - I frankly don't see how - we landed a plane - in the driving rain - or took off from that pitching bow...but we made it somehow."

*   *   *   *   *

The last training assignment for our squadron before going overseas, was flying to an airbase outside of 29 Palms, California, .for a weekend. This was a small community in those days, now a major Marine base, but there were cottages for married officers so Kay and some of the other wives drove over.

The field was plain dessert, bulldozed flat then covered with a Marston Mat. This was like a heavy and closely woven link fence. It stretched one way - West to East - for the prevailing winds, .and it was wide enough for an unusual take-off of four planes at the same time. I think this was to allow faster operations. So when it was time for our four-plane division, we roared down the mat and into the air in formation on our division leader. We landed one at a time.

The main objective of this program was to learn how to handle "Tiny Tim". Tim was a 2000 pound bomb. Since we were a fighter / BOMBER squadron, this baby was for us. It was like a small aerial torpedo, with fins that insured a steady flight to the target. Probably the father of today's fancy guided and heat-seeking missiles.

Tim was attached under our plane's bellies, and of course was unarmed for practice. We had a target and fired our bomb as if it were a Jap ship. Only one of our stalwarts shot his Tim early and it landed just outside the town. No one was injured, but this pilot got hell.

As long as we were there, the Navy figured, we might as well learn some other aggressive moves, like strafing with real bullets. We had made dummy runs before, but this was actually firing our four .50 caliber, wing-mounted machine guns at targets on the ground. Pretty exciting for guys preparing for action in the Pacific.

And we practiced with side arms on land, firing .45 caliber automatics while walking up to the target. The shooting war seemed to be getting closer.

There was also a riding stable in the town, and Kay and I thought it would be fun to see the hills of the desert from horseback on my free time. The ponies were friendly. They had two speeds...a walk away from the barn, and a gallop home. Once was enough.

* * * * *

The other carrier training, when we were stationed on the island of Maui, was at night aboard the semi-retired carrier, USS SARATOGA. To prepare for this adventure, we practiced at night on a simulated carrier deck (like Jacksonville) on the near end of Hilo, the Big Isle. We all qualified. By now the procedure was like parking a car.

The division and section leaders (including me) were to fly our planes aboard the SARATOGA. The Navy normally scheduled these drills on full moon nights. That was the forecast for us, but at the time of take-off, clouds began to form and by the time we found the ship it was a full overcast.

Our squadron, landed safely but the commander of the Torpedo Squadron in our air group was not so lucky. He came in too hot, his plane missed the last wire and he crashed into the control tower. The deck gang was on the plane in an instant, pulled the pilot out safely and pushed the damaged plane over the side.

Operations finally began. We were to make three take-offs and landings. My first take-off was almost my last. I was on the catapult, ready to go with full power on and the tail up. I signaled the catapult officer, on the right side of the plane, that I was all set by bringing my left arm across my chest. Then I put my left hand back on the throttle and the "hold" device (so the forward force wouldn't pull the throttle back). The signal officer threw his right arm toward the bow to signal "go" and I was off.

Maybe half way down the catapult I knew I wouldn't make it. Thank God for my catapult training back at Corpus, where I had five "shots". . I pulled the throttle back and jammed on the brakes. The nose plowed into the deck about 50 feet from the bow. Shit, if I'm wrong, it's probably a courts martial. But the catapult officer jumped up on the wing and said:" You're a lucky bastard. That was a half shot. You'd have been shark bait".

* * * * *

Another interesting drill in the islands seemed like fun and games. The uniform was bathing suits and a sweatshirt top. We were taken a few miles offshore in a Navy tug. Then with an inflatable one-man float boat strapped to our bottoms, we were over the side into the rather warm Pacific. Obviously, this was practice for a forced landing, assuming you ditched safely and crawled out of the cockpit in one piece, or parachuted. The head officer on the tug said they'd pick us up in about a half hour. All the little lifeboats inflated properly.

With maybe 15 knots of wind, the 18 VBF-14 pilots were scattered widely. I was the last one to be rescued. The splashing water over the raft for almost two hours was hypnotic…and ultimately hypothermic. When the tug finally found me, I couldn't hold onto the rescue line they threw. One of my buddies dove in and pulled me alongside. Fortunately, there was brandy aboard the tug for just such a problem.

*   *   *   *   *

Our fighter / bomber squadron was part of Air Group 14. It also included a fighter squadron of F4Fs, dive-bomber SBDs, and torpedo bomber TBFs. We were ordered to the Hawaiian Islands to go aboard CV 11…the INTREPID. We would leave from San Francisco as passengers aboard the CV BENNINGTON. Most of us spent our last two days in California in the Top of the Mark (the Mark Hopkins hotel).

It was a little teary and very drunky. Kay and I had our last dinner at Trader Vic's and a passionate love feast for God knows how long. We talked about how wonderful life would be when the war was finally over. No thought of any other possibility.

She drove home to Wichita with another wife and we headed out to sea. A Chief Petty Officer was standing next to me on the flight deck when we went under the Golden Gate Bridge. There was a crowd of young women in skirts waving us on. He said: "Take your last look. You wont see it again for months…if ever".

As a squadron - we were charmed, you might say. Twice we were packed and scheduled to board the INTREPID. The first time was delayed because the carrier took a Jap torpedo in the series off Turk Island, and was out of action temporarily for repairs at Pearl Harbor. We were held over on the Kahalui base on the island of Maui. We were trained and ready for combat, but this life could be beautiful.

My roommate and good friend was my Division leader, Lt. Bob Bender. He had been an alternate running back at Iowa and his one great claim to fame was starting the Notre Dame Game. This was his second tour of duty; his first was as a dive-bomber on the WASP, and unfortunately for Bob, the seductive French / Polynesian beauty of his earlier trip to Hawaii was otherwise Involved this time around.

After six days of practice we could take turns and fly into Honolulu for three days. My good friend Bill Wilson had friends on Oahu, where we could spend the night. There was surfing and MaiTais and beach parties and friendly young natives to swim with at night. Bill and I were good body surfers so we thought using rented surfboards would be similar and relatively easy. Not so. These early boards were big and heavy mothers. Maybe in two hours we caught three waves. We were too proud or stupid to take lessons.

*   *   *   *   *

On one of my return hops from Honolulu to Maui, usually routine, my engine began to sputter. No normal procedure helped. Suddenly my first thought was that I didn't want to put this expensive plane in the drink if I didn't make it back to base. Then I realized what I really didn't want to do was swim with the sharks, if I got out of the plane alive.

So I made a rather skittish landing on the emergency runway on an island halfway home, Molokai. I called the base on the radio and they said they would send a mechanic and told me not to get out of your plane. Then I remembered this was still a last ditch home for a colony of lepers. It must have seemed weird to them for me to be sitting in the cockpit and doing nothing.

The local folks were standing by, waiting. I pointed to the engine, and gestured with my hand across my throat. Heads nodded .I didn't see any obvious symptoms, like in that section of the movie, Ben Hur, but I felt it would be unkind to stare. They gradually faded away and the rescue plane fixed my problem.

The USS INTREPID

This historic aircraft carrier survived two severe enemy attacks in WWII, and served in two more wars. Now a magnificent museum on the Hudson River in NYC, Official US Navy Photograph from Naval Historical Center

Finally the INTREPID came out of dry dock at Pearl and we went aboard. Our immediate destination was the island of Guam. We flew every other day and really learned wartime carrier procedures

On these "search and report" missions, our basic navigation was dead reckoning, using a "plotting board" which fit under our instrument panel. We would record our heading, time, speed, estimated drift angle, and estimated distance covered on each leg of our mission. Of course there was nothing important to see as the war had moved far west! Maybe a Jap sub had strayed away from its base, but we didn't find it!

CONSOLAN was our radio support. Primitive compared to today's systems, but effective. The ship issued a coded signal, over 360 degree divided into 15 degree segments, so you knew where you were relative to the INTREPID, and could easily conclude whether the ship was getting closer or farther away by the strength of the signal. The code was changed every day.

The author on board the INTREPID, on his F4U with folded wings ready for
stowage below on the hangar deck.

Life on board when we weren't flying or on stand-by was a mix of phys / ed, lots of poker, gin rummy, acey-ducey (a backgammon derivative) and reading. The INTREPID had a fine library. My favorite books were documentaries about defense lawyers who went to great lengths to help their clients. I knew that the Law was for me.

Without a degree from Northwestern I felt my chances for enrolling in law school post war were minimal, but I wrote my most appealing letter - to who else but – Harvard. Of course this was like shooting an arrow into the air. Actually it fell to earth on a wonderful admission department. They wrote back and said to call when I got home and they would work me in somehow!

It was not to happen. A strange family tragedy changed my future. When I returned to the States, and to Kay in Wichita, my aging mother called and said you and Kay must fly to Palm Beach - right now. Your sister has a serious problem, her husband Steve is believed to be somewhere in the Chesapeake Bay! The Navy thinks she should come to Washington, now. The prospects are grim. Her two little boys are your nephews and you have to care for them.

The full story centered on what was called "basket leave". The twin Beech's pilot was flying a group of officers to Palm Beach (Steve's home) for a little fun and escape from DC duties. If everything went smoothly, the leave papers would be torn up and the leave would not count. If not, the flight was "official". Things did not go as planned.

Near Dulles airport in DC, the thunderheads were so severe that the twin Beech had to circle the airport for a chance to land. Finally the tower told them to turn back to Richmond. The pilot said he was low on fuel. (He had a date in DC and had not stopped to refuel.) They never made it.

The engines quit when they were over the Bay. The pilot didn't know exactly where they were. He told his passengers, equipped with chutes, their best bet was to jump. Of the seven men on board, fishermen found four lucky guys. Steve Dechman was not found alive. Several days later, when Lorraine was in Washington, his body was washed ashore.

When she came back to Palm Beach she was almost beyond help. We stayed a month until, with help of friends; she was somewhat able to think about her kids and the future. I missed my chance for entrance to Harvard. I realized that it would have been very difficult at best – married, with limited funds, and no family or friends in Boston. Then Northwestern turned me down, without completing undergraduate work, so I decided that my future would be in the unknown world of business. I never made the law.

Now our youngest, David, is a high profile attorney who has just been certified to practice before the US Supreme Court. Maybe the genes were always there, anyway. Our other son, George III (aka Chip) is now a successful cargo ship broker and daughter Ellary is becoming star in the film production business in Hollywood.

* * * * *

Another surprise greeted us when we arrived in Guam aboard the INTREPID. The Navy decided that the previous air group had not logged the usual 6 months at sea. They were ordered back on the ship and we were put ashore for the second time! This time to Marpi Point on the neighboring island of Saipan. .

The very unhappy guys in Air Group 19 (I think it was 19) were so pissed off about this new order that they hacked down all the plants grown carefully by the very unpopular base commander, called "Black Barnie". He in turn closed the primitive O club on us. And he had all our personal baggage checked for booze. The word of this wicked action passed quickly, so I hid several illicit bottles of Scotch. One I traded later to a SEABEE (Naval construction engineer) for a Japanese sword. Our skipper, with his track record with the fleet, managed to get the O club reopened.

Waiting our turn to go back on the INTREPID was dull duty. Movies at night were outdoors. Occasionally, Japs hiding in the hills would shoot at us. No casualties.

Now it is August. It seems ironic, after months of training to win the war, and once having orders to map Japan, that when the bomb was dropped on Hiroshima, I was playing gin rummy in the Ready Room on Saipan.

Then we hit Nagasaki. VJ Day was August 15, 1945. Our war, in the Pacific, was over. Some of our Air Group went back on the INTREPID and sailed into Tokyo Bay. I had enough "points" to go home and my VJ day would be with Kathryn J, as in Jane, in Wichita. My almost four years of duty were over. I repeat, I was one fortunate FLY BOY. I often think of the heroes who fought in the Pacific on ships and islands and especially, of the soldiers who toughed it out on Omaha Beach and beyond in that other war. May God be with them. He was good to me.

*　　*　　*　　*　　*

The ship that brought me home from Guam was an ex-United Fruit transport. As guest officers our quarters and privileges were limited. There was a small Wardroom and Hearts was the game of choice. Fresh water was limited and we could shower only every other day from 3 to 4. One afternoon I had just "Shot the moon", and forgot about the time restraint. With 15 minutes left, I headed to my cabin to grab a towel, and raced for the shower. With Soap from head to foot and feeling wonderfully clean, I was ready to rinse when, you guessed it, the water stopped. What the hell to do.

I was standing in the companionway when a Chief Petty Officer came by, "Excuse me, sir, I think I can help". (How did he know I was an officer?) "Follow me, you'll use the Chiefs' shower". I'm sure God smiles on Chiefs!

*   *   *   *   *

As we neared San Francisco I knew that my six months of chastity would be over soon… or maybe sooner. At the dock were hundreds of cheering women, to greet the ship's crew and guests, or simply speculating. Although the war had been over for a couple of months, it was the first chance all of us on the ship had to cheer the victory at home. Scenes like that famous Eichenlaub picture in LIFE of the sailor *REALLY* kissing the nurse on Broadway in N YC were repeated right here and now. The spirit was contagious.

There was a kiosk to help with hotels. A fellow VBF-14 pilot and I booked the Sir France Drake in the center of town. It was about 9 PM and after taking our bags upstairs, we ordered ice and had a drink. Then we decided we really weren't so tired after all and decided to check out the lounge.

Here it was Katy-Bar-The-Door! Lots of clinking ice cubes and laughs from dozens of young couples and singles. The girls were flirting and the guys in uniform were hugging and snuggling. I heard a sexy voice say: "I'll take the tall one". Since I was a little taller I thought we might be the targets. You bet! After two drinks and lots of small talk and cozy looks, we headed upstairs - where it wouldn't be so noisy.

A drink in the room and the social foursome morphed into two amorous couples. God it felt good to hold a woman close. Fortunately, I suppose, because I had been straight arrow and free love had not yet come to San Francisco, there was a knock on the door, the lock was turned, and a house dick joined the party.

"Sorry guys, hotel rules, you'll have to break it up. I'll wait outside". In a single moment the mood had turned from warm and loving to cold and sober. The game was here, and the whistle blew. The girls tidied up, blew a kiss, and took off.

The next day I landed a TWA flight, but only as far as Oklahoma City. The plane's Captain was told I wanted to go on to Wichita. He saw my wings and said: "Come up here with us. You'll be our Navigator to Wichita."

With a little help from the pilot's radio, Kay met the plane and it was almost unbelievable that we were finally back together at the same airport where we had first met two years ago. My FLY BOY days were over. Our lovemaking that night was intense. The war was over and our romance was almost like it was just beginning. We hoped that this would be the start of a totally new and exciting life together. And it was.

EPILOGUE

Suddenly I wake up and realize I'm a civilian and need a job. I answer an ad in the Chicago Tribune for a Sales Management Trainee at the Parker Pen Co. Everybody wanted a Parker 51, so it must be a solid company. I am invited to interview in Janesville, Wisconsin. Janesville? It's on the map near Madison so we hop in the old V-8.

I park in front of the impressive building and tell Kay to drive around and check out the town and nearby neighborhoods. After an hour I climb back in the car and ask Kay how she liked the place. She said: "I wouldn't be caught dead here!"

My sad reply: "Well, you'll get used to it, the job sounded swell and I took it!"

We didn't talk on the way back to Chicago, but I told her about the great life (which they had told me) in a small town and we made up that night.

Here is where we spent ten years, brought three children into the world. (The OB Charged me $125 for the third one and I told him to stop raising his prices!) Mercy Hospital and the Sisters were so thoughtful I almost converted. And in this very conventional town; we built a one-story redwood house with slanted roofs, and radiant heating. It was designed by Frank Lloyd Wright's best student and ended up in Better Homes and Gardens.

We joined the Country Club, made many friends, learned the local sport - shooting geese, ducks and pheasants, and raised a wonderful hunting dog. And I grew into the job of Advertising Manager at Parker. It was a nice life.

*   *   *   *   *

But life changes. Parker bought the Eversharp Pen Co. and set up shop outside Chicago in the suburb of Lincolnwood. I was appointed Marketing VP.and we moved to Kenilworth on the North Shore of Lake Michigan, near where I had grown up. Sadly, business didn't develop as planned, Eversharp was moved to Janesville – without me.

Happily, I scored with Bell and Howell and became Product Manager for 8mm cameras (remember movie cameras?) and Director of Amateur Film for a project with DuPont that never flew .But after a successful decade, Kay wanted to leave the suburbs with their PTAs and Garden Clubs. She was becoming a successful artist with many awards and wanted the stimulating and challenging life of a big city. I had a chance to become Executive VP of a small company in NYC. I took it.

The firm was Party Tyme. Not a call girl ring or event planner, but the developers of a cocktail mix product. Just add ice and booze to the shaker we provided and you had Bloody Marys or Whiskey Sours or Mai Tais. A huge success. After three years I headed up an IPO and we were going to be rich.

It was not to be, the SEC pronounced our "red herring" issue a miserable investment and the company was eventually sold to Seagrams. The reason for this total turn around was basically a new *POWDERED* drink mix, called Bartender's,. In a little envelope, It was easy to stock and display and carry home and it made a good drink. We just couldn't compete.

*   *   *   *   *

Finally, life turns around again. Kay becomes the founder of an exciting craft gallery, and I enter the magazine business to ultimately become Publisher of SAILING WORLD, devoted primarily to racing sailors. Quite a switch from golf and tennis, but my focus had been changing to the big blue sea and the challenge of racing and cruising sailboats.

Kay's craft gallery, called the Elements, actually started in Greenwich CT. It was a showplace that we modified from an old stable, and with both of us working in CT we moved from NYC to a storied house on a creek with a waterfall and a natural swimming pool. Later, with more partners, she opened a successful branch on Madison Avenue in NYC.

For twenty years, my days with SAILING WORLD were fantastic. We were the first Americans to sail to Cuba after Castro took charge. And in the first Sardinia Cup, I headed a three boat Canadian team (my grandmother was a French Canadian so I qualified) to Porto Cervo. There were 14 countries competing. It was a fabulous week.

My own 39' WINDANCE was First to Finish in our class on the famous 640-mile Newport RI to Bermuda race. We were given a hero's welcome at the Royal Bermuda Yacht Club with band music and hugs and kisses from the women on a dock that was reserved for class winners. But another skipper, the legendary sailboat designer and racer, Ted Hood, had slipped in ahead of us and moored around the corner of the harbor at the Royal Canoe Club. He welcomed us, quietly, in his blue blazer Oh well, second to Ted after five days on the ocean wasn't too bad.

One final event was as frightening as any of my FLY BOY challenges… our New York Yacht Club overnight race from the Cape Cod Canal to Camden Maine. The fog was so intense that we could barely see the bow of our boat. All we could hear were the foghorns of ocean freighters passing very close in front or behind us They must have been watching Radar. This was before hi-tech navigation instruments for sailboats. We survived and went on win the week-long racing cruise.

Obviously I remember the success stories - there were others!

* * * * *

In the late 80s, SAILING WORLD was sold to the New York Times, and moved to Newport RI. I retired, Kay sold her business, and we moved to California. The San Francisco Bay area is a wonderful place to recall all these adventures. Our house in the Oakland hills was fantastic, a view of Mt. Diablo over park lands to the East, and the Bay looking to the West. But for the last two years we have been in the special section of Aegis Assisted Living called Life's Neighborhood, where Kay receives extra help as needed, and I struggle with my own aging memory and a new computer..

Finally, it's been a good life, however long it may last!

* * * * *

Post Script... A special thanks to my creative filmmaker daughter, Ellary, for her editing support and incredible skill in processing photos on this Macintosh, and to Karl Schroeder, my long-suffering Author's Representative at Outskirts Press for his assistance in bringing FLY BOY to press.

Now I would like to dedicate this memoir to Kathryn Jane Corbett Eddy who bumped me off that Braniff DC-3 in 1943 for a priority passenger, succumbed to my charms, and has shared her love and many talents with me ever since.

And to the Alzheimer's Associates, I will contribute any financial gain from this book.

Lightning Source UK Ltd.
Milton Keynes UK
UKOW051642110612

194237UK00001B/298/A